My Favorite Sports

I LOVE GYMNASTICS

By Ryan Nagelhout

Gareth Stevens
PUBLISHING

Please visit our website, www.garethstevens.com. For a free color catalog of all our high-quality books, call toll free 1-800-542-2595 or fax 1-877-542-2596.

Library of Congress Cataloging-in-Publication Data

Nagelhout, Ryan.
I love gymnastics / by Ryan Nagelhout.
p. cm. — (My favorite sports)
Includes index.
ISBN 978-1-4824-0730-3 (pbk.)
ISBN 978-1-4824-0770-9 (6-pack)
ISBN 978-1-4824-0728-0 (library binding)
1. Gymnastics — Juvenile literature. I. Nagelhout, Ryan. II. Title.
GV461.3 N34 2015
796.44—d23

First Edition

Published in 2015 by
Gareth Stevens Publishing
111 East 14th Street, Suite 349
New York, NY 10003

Copyright © 2015 Gareth Stevens Publishing

Editor: Ryan Nagelhout
Designer: Nick Domiano

Photo credits: Cover, p. 1 Katkov/iStock/Thinkstock.com; p. 5 Jupiterimages/BananaStock/Thinkstock.com; p. 7 David Handley/Dorling Kindersley/Getty Images; p. 9, 24 (flip) Tony Wear/Shutterstock.com; p. 13 Amana Images/Thinkstock.com; p. 11 Assembly/Photographer's Choice RF/Getty Images; p. 13 Fuse/Fuse/Getty Images; pp. 15, 24 (mat) Micha Klootwijk/Shutterstock.com; pp. 17, 19 Michael C. Gray/Shutterstock.com; pp. 21, 24 (roll) Alexey Fursov/Shutterstock.com; p. 23 alexkatkov/Shutterstock.com.

Printed in the United States of America

CPSIA compliance information: Batch #CS15GS: For further information contact Gareth Stevens, New York, New York at 1-800-542-2595.

Contents

Roll and Flip 4

Safety First. 12

Loosen Up! 16

New Moves 20

Words to Know 24

Index. 24

It is time for gymnastics!

I learn how to roll.
This is called tumbling.

7

I learn how to do flips.

I do not wear
any socks.

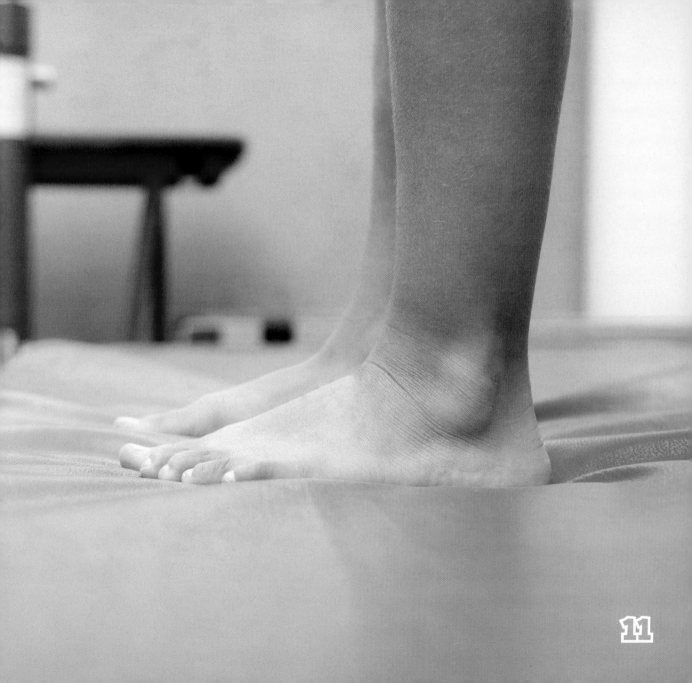

11

I put down mats.

The mats keep me safe.

You need to keep your body loose.

17

You have to be strong!

19

I love to learn
new things.

Come train with us!

23

Words to Know

flip

mat

roll

Index

flips 8

safe 14

mats 12, 14

tumbling 6

24